THIS TEACHER PLANNER BELONGS TO:

TEACHER *Information*

CLASS #:   SCHOOL:

GRADE: ADDRESS:

SCHOOL YEAR: PHONE:

NOTES & MEMOS

RESOURCE LINKS

PERSONAL NOTES

SCHOOL Holidays

AUGUST

SEPTEMBER

OCTOBER

NOVEMBER

DECEMBER

NOTES

SCHOOL *Holidays*

JANUARY

FEBRUARY

MARCH

APRIL

MAY

JUNE

NOTES:

YEAR AT A *Glance*

AUGUST	SEPTEMBER	OCTOBER
NOVEMBER	**DECEMBER**	**JANUARY**
FEBRUARY	**MARCH**	**APRIL**
MAY	**JUNE**	

NOTES:

PARENT *Contacts*

STUDENT:

PARENTS:

PHONE #:

EMAIL:

STUDENT:

PARENTS:

PHONE #:

EMAIL:

STUDENT:

PARENTS:

PHONE #:

EMAIL:

STUDENT:

PARENTS:

PHONE #:

EMAIL:

STUDENT:

PARENTS:

PHONE #:

EMAIL:

STUDENT:

PARENTS:

PHONE #:

EMAIL:

STUDENT:

PARENTS:

PHONE #:

EMAIL:

STUDENT:

PARENTS:

PHONE #:

EMAIL:

STUDENT:

PARENTS:

PHONE #:

EMAIL:

STUDENT:

PARENTS:

PHONE #:

EMAIL:

PARENT *Contacts*

STUDENT:	STUDENT:
PARENTS:	PARENTS:
PHONE #:	PHONE #:
EMAIL:	EMAIL:
STUDENT:	STUDENT:
PARENTS:	PARENTS:
PHONE #:	PHONE #:
EMAIL:	EMAIL:
STUDENT:	STUDENT:
PARENTS:	PARENTS:
PHONE #:	PHONE #:
EMAIL:	EMAIL:
STUDENT:	STUDENT:
PARENTS:	PARENTS:
PHONE #:	PHONE #:
EMAIL:	EMAIL:
STUDENT:	STUDENT:
PARENTS:	PARENTS:
PHONE #:	PHONE #:
EMAIL:	EMAIL:

PARENT *Contacts*

STUDENT:

PARENTS:

PHONE #:

EMAIL:

STUDENT:

PARENTS:

PHONE #:

EMAIL:

STUDENT:

PARENTS:

PHONE #:

EMAIL:

STUDENT:

PARENTS:

PHONE #:

EMAIL:

STUDENT:

PARENTS:

PHONE #:

EMAIL:

STUDENT:

PARENTS:

PHONE #:

EMAIL:

STUDENT:

PARENTS:

PHONE #:

EMAIL:

STUDENT:

PARENTS:

PHONE #:

EMAIL:

STUDENT:

PARENTS:

PHONE #:

EMAIL:

STUDENT:

PARENTS:

PHONE #:

EMAIL:

PARENT CONTACT *Log*

MONTH:

NAME & DATE:	REASON:	METHOD:	NOTES:
		EMAIL:	
		PHONE:	
		MEETING:	

DATE:	REASON:	METHOD:	NOTES:
		EMAIL:	
		PHONE:	
		MEETING:	

DATE:	REASON:	METHOD:	NOTES:
		EMAIL:	
		PHONE:	
		MEETING:	

DATE:	REASON:	METHOD:	NOTES:
		EMAIL:	
		PHONE:	
		MEETING:	

DATE:	REASON:	METHOD:	NOTES:
		EMAIL:	
		PHONE:	
		MEETING:	

NOTES

PARENT CONTACT *Log*

MONTH:

NAME & DATE:	REASON:	METHOD:	NOTES:
		EMAIL:	
		PHONE:	
		MEETING:	

DATE:	REASON:	METHOD:	NOTES:
		EMAIL:	
		PHONE:	
		MEETING:	

DATE:	REASON:	METHOD:	NOTES:
		EMAIL:	
		PHONE:	
		MEETING:	

DATE:	REASON:	METHOD:	NOTES:
		EMAIL:	
		PHONE:	
		MEETING:	

DATE:	REASON:	METHOD:	NOTES:
		EMAIL:	
		PHONE:	
		MEETING:	

NOTES

PARENT CONTACT *Log*

MONTH:

NAME & DATE:	REASON:	METHOD:	NOTES:
		EMAIL:	
		PHONE:	
		MEETING:	

DATE:	REASON:	METHOD:	NOTES:
		EMAIL:	
		PHONE:	
		MEETING:	

DATE:	REASON:	METHOD:	NOTES:
		EMAIL:	
		PHONE:	
		MEETING:	

DATE:	REASON:	METHOD:	NOTES:
		EMAIL:	
		PHONE:	
		MEETING:	

DATE:	REASON:	METHOD:	NOTES:
		EMAIL:	
		PHONE:	
		MEETING:	

NOTES

PARENT CONTACT *Log*

MONTH:

NAME & DATE:	REASON:	METHOD:	NOTES:
		EMAIL:	
		PHONE:	
		MEETING:	

DATE:	REASON:	METHOD:	NOTES:
		EMAIL:	
		PHONE:	
		MEETING:	

DATE:	REASON:	METHOD:	NOTES:
		EMAIL:	
		PHONE:	
		MEETING:	

DATE:	REASON:	METHOD:	NOTES:
		EMAIL:	
		PHONE:	
		MEETING:	

DATE:	REASON:	METHOD:	NOTES:
		EMAIL:	
		PHONE:	
		MEETING:	

NOTES

PARENT CONTACT *Log*

MONTH:

NAME & DATE:	REASON:	METHOD:	NOTES:
		EMAIL:	
		PHONE:	
		MEETING:	

DATE:	REASON:	METHOD:	NOTES:
		EMAIL:	
		PHONE:	
		MEETING:	

DATE:	REASON:	METHOD:	NOTES:
		EMAIL:	
		PHONE:	
		MEETING:	

DATE:	REASON:	METHOD:	NOTES:
		EMAIL:	
		PHONE:	
		MEETING:	

DATE:	REASON:	METHOD:	NOTES:
		EMAIL:	
		PHONE:	
		MEETING:	

NOTES

PARENT CONTACT *Log*

MONTH:

NAME & DATE:	REASON:	METHOD:	NOTES:
		EMAIL:	
		PHONE:	
		MEETING:	

DATE:	REASON:	METHOD:	NOTES:
		EMAIL:	
		PHONE:	
		MEETING:	

DATE:	REASON:	METHOD:	NOTES:
		EMAIL:	
		PHONE:	
		MEETING:	

DATE:	REASON:	METHOD:	NOTES:
		EMAIL:	
		PHONE:	
		MEETING:	

DATE:	REASON:	METHOD:	NOTES:
		EMAIL:	
		PHONE:	
		MEETING:	

NOTES

STUDENT *Birthdays*

AUGUST

SEPTEMBER

OCTOBER

NOVEMBER

DECEMBER

JANUARY

FEBRUARY

MARCH

APRIL

MAY

JUNE

CLASSROOM *Expenses*

MONTH: **YEAR:**

CLASS:

DATE	ITEM	DESCRIPTION	CATEGORY	COST

DATE:

CLASS Field Trip

EVENT

DATE:

LOCATION

TIME

DEPT TIME:

TOTAL COST:

RETURN TIME:

CONTACT

FIELD TRIP Checklist

☐	☐
☐	☐
☐	☐
☐	☐
☐	☐
☐	☐
☐	☐
☐	☐
☐	☐
☐	

IMPORTANT Reminders

Field Trip Itinerary

TIME:	ACTIVITIES:

PROGRESS *Report*

CLASS/SUBJECT:

DATE	SUBJECT/CLASS	LESSON PLAN #	ASSIGNMENTS

NOTES & IDEAS

ASSESSMENT

CUSTOMIZED ACTION PLAN

ASSIGNMENT *Tracker*

CLASS/SUBJECT: ————————————— WEEK OF: —————————————

MONDAY:	TUESDAY	WEDNESDAY

THURSDAY	FRIDAY	NOTES:

READING *Tracker*

CLASS:

BOOK TITLE: AUTHOR:

DATE	STUDENT	PAGES READ	NOTES

MONTHLY *Notes*

AUGUST				
M	T	W	T	F

NOTES, ACTIVITIES, PLANS & IDEAS

MONTHLY *Schedule*

CLASSROOM: **MONTH:**

M	T	W	T	F	S	S

NOTES, ACTIVITIES, PLANS & IDEAS

MONTHLY *Notes*

SEPTEMBER				
M	T	W	T	F

NOTES, ACTIVITIES, PLANS & IDEAS

MONTHLY *Schedule*

CLASSROOM: **MONTH:**

M	T	W	T	F	S	S

NOTES, ACTIVITIES, PLANS & IDEAS

MONTHLY *Notes*

OCTOBER

M	T	W	T	F

NOTES, ACTIVITIES, PLANS & IDEAS

MONTHLY *Schedule*

CLASSROOM: **MONTH:**

M	T	W	T	F	S	S

NOTES, ACTIVITIES, PLANS & IDEAS

MONTHLY *Notes*

NOVEMBER				
M	T	W	T	F

NOTES, ACTIVITIES, PLANS & IDEAS

MONTHLY *Schedule*

CLASSROOM: **MONTH:**

M	T	W	T	F	S	S

NOTES, ACTIVITIES, PLANS & IDEAS

MONTHLY *Notes*

DECEMBER

M	T	W	T	F

NOTES, ACTIVITIES, PLANS & IDEAS

MONTHLY *Schedule*

CLASSROOM: **MONTH:**

M	T	W	T	F	S	S

NOTES, ACTIVITIES, PLANS & IDEAS

MONTHLY *Notes*

JANUARY				
M	T	W	T	F

NOTES, ACTIVITIES, PLANS & IDEAS

MONTHLY Schedule

CLASSROOM: **MONTH:**

M	T	W	T	F	S	S

NOTES, ACTIVITIES, PLANS & IDEAS

MONTHLY *Notes*

FEBRUARY				
M	T	W	T	F

NOTES, ACTIVITIES, PLANS & IDEAS

MONTHLY *Schedule*

CLASSROOM: **MONTH:**

M	T	W	T	F	S	S

NOTES, ACTIVITIES, PLANS & IDEAS

MONTHLY *Notes*

		MARCH		
M	T	W	T	F

NOTES, ACTIVITIES, PLANS & IDEAS

MONTHLY Schedule

CLASSROOM: **MONTH:**

M	T	W	T	F	S	S

NOTES, ACTIVITIES, PLANS & IDEAS

MONTHLY Notes

	APRIL			
M	T	W	T	F

NOTES, ACTIVITIES, PLANS & IDEAS

MONTHLY *Schedule*

CLASSROOM: **MONTH:**

M	T	W	T	F	S	S

NOTES, ACTIVITIES, PLANS & IDEAS

MONTHLY *Notes*

		MAY		
M	T	W	T	F

NOTES, ACTIVITIES, PLANS & IDEAS

MONTHLY *Schedule*

CLASSROOM: **MONTH:**

M	T	W	T	F	S	S

NOTES, ACTIVITIES, PLANS & IDEAS

MONTHLY *Notes*

JUNE				
M	T	W	T	F

NOTES, ACTIVITIES, PLANS & IDEAS

MONTHLY *Schedule*

CLASSROOM: **MONTH:**

M	T	W	T	F	S	S

NOTES, ACTIVITIES, PLANS & IDEAS

DATE:

WEEKLY ROLL *Call*

FIRST NAME:	LAST NAME:	STATUS:

WEEKLY *Overview*

WEEK OF: ....

MONDAY	TUESDAY	WEDNESDAY

THURSDAY	FRIDAY	SATURDAY

SUNDAY

IMPORTANT NOTES

WEEKLY *Lesson Plan*

MONDAY

EQ/ I CAN NOTES:

TUESDAY

EQ/ I CAN NOTES:

WEDNESDAY

EQ/ I CAN NOTES:

THURSDAY

EQ/ I CAN NOTES:

FRIDAY

EQ/ I CAN NOTES:

CLASS *Projects*

PROJECT TITLE: **DETAILS:**

START DATE: **DUE DATE:**

DATE   **TASK COMPLETED**

READING *Tracker*

CLASS: ....

| BOOK TITLE: | AUTHOR: |

DATE	STUDENT	PAGES READ	NOTES

WEEKLY *Planner*

MONDAY

TUESDAY

WEDNESDAY

THURSDAY

FRIDAY

EQ/I CAN NOTES:

LESSON *Planner*

SUBJECT:

UNIT:

LESSON:

DATE:

OBJECTIVE:

OVERVIEW

TOPICS COVERED

ASSIGNMENTS

NOTES

ASSIGNMENT *Tracker*

CLASS/SUBJECT: _____   WEEK OF: _____

MONDAY:	TUESDAY	WEDNESDAY

THURSDAY	FRIDAY	NOTES:

DAILY Schedule

TO DO LIST:

DATE ....

6 AM

7 AM

8 AM

9 AM

10 AM

11 AM

12 PM

1 PM

2 PM

3 PM

4 PM

5 PM

REMINDERS:

6 PM

7 PM

8 PM

9 PM

10 PM

NOTES:

NOTES

DAY PLANNER *Monday*

DATE:

5am:

6am:

7am:

8am:

9am:

10am:

11am:

12pm:

1pm:

2pm:

3pm:

4pm:

DAILY TO DO LIST:

DAILY GOALS:

NOTES & REMINDERS:

DAY PLANNER  Tuesday

DATE:

DAILY TO DO LIST:

5am:

6am:

7am:

8am: **DAILY GOALS:**

9am:

10am:

11am:

NOTES & REMINDERS:

12pm:

1pm:

2pm:

3pm:

4pm:

DAY PLANNER *Wednesday*

DATE:

5am:

6am:

7am:

8am:

9am:

10am:

11am:

12pm:

1pm:

2pm:

3pm:

4pm:

DAILY TO DO LIST:

DAILY GOALS:

NOTES & REMINDERS:

DAY PLANNER *Thursday*

DATE:

5am:

6am:

7am:

8am:

9am:

10am:

11am:

12pm:

1pm:

2pm:

3pm:

4pm:

DAILY TO DO LIST:

DAILY GOALS:

NOTES & REMINDERS:

DAY PLANNER

DATE:

5am:

6am:

7am:

8am:

9am:

10am:

11am:

12pm:

1pm:

2pm:

3pm:

4pm:

DAILY TO DO LIST:

DAILY GOALS:

NOTES & REMINDERS:

DATE:

WEEKLY ROLL *Call*

FIRST NAME: LAST NAME: STATUS:

WEEKLY *Overview*

WEEK OF: ....

MONDAY

TUESDAY

WEDNESDAY

THURSDAY

FRIDAY

SATURDAY

SUNDAY

IMPORTANT NOTES

WEEKLY *Lesson Plan*

MONDAY

EQ/ I CAN NOTES:

TUESDAY

EQ/ I CAN NOTES:

WEDNESDAY

EQ/ I CAN NOTES:

THURSDAY

EQ/ I CAN NOTES:

FRIDAY

EQ/ I CAN NOTES:

READING *Tracker*

CLASS: ....

BOOK TITLE: .... AUTHOR: ....

DATE	STUDENT	PAGES READ	NOTES

LESSON *Planner*

SUBJECT:

UNIT:

LESSON:

DATE:

OBJECTIVE:

OVERVIEW

TOPICS COVERED

ASSIGNMENTS

NOTES

DAY PLANNER *Monday*

DATE:

DAILY TO DO LIST:

5am:

6am:

7am:

8am:
                                        DAILY GOALS:

9am:

10am:

11am:
                            NOTES & REMINDERS:

12pm:

1pm:

2pm:

3pm:

4pm:

DAY PLANNER  *Tuesday*

DATE:

5am:

6am:

7am:

8am:

9am:

10am:

11am:

12pm:

1pm:

2pm:

3pm:

4pm:

DAILY TO DO LIST:

DAILY GOALS:

NOTES & REMINDERS:

DAY PLANNER *Wednesday*

DATE:

5am:

6am:

7am:

8am:

9am:

10am:

11am:

12pm:

1pm:

2pm:

3pm:

4pm:

DAILY TO DO LIST:

DAILY GOALS:

NOTES & REMINDERS:

DAY PLANNER *Thursday*

DATE:

5am:

6am:

7am:

8am:

9am:

10am:

11am:

12pm:

1pm:

2pm:

3pm:

4pm:

DAILY TO DO LIST:

DAILY GOALS:

NOTES & REMINDERS:

DAY PLANNER

DATE:

5am:

6am:

7am:

8am:

9am:

10am:

11am:

12pm:

1pm:

2pm:

3pm:

4pm:

DAILY TO DO LIST:

DAILY GOALS:

NOTES & REMINDERS:

DATE:

WEEKLY ROLL *Call*

FIRST NAME: LAST NAME: STATUS:

WEEKLY *Overview*

WEEK OF: ....

MONDAY

TUESDAY

WEDNESDAY

THURSDAY

FRIDAY

SATURDAY

SUNDAY

IMPORTANT NOTES

WEEKLY *Lesson Plan*

MONDAY

EQ/ I CAN NOTES:

TUESDAY

EQ/ I CAN NOTES:

WEDNESDAY

EQ/ I CAN NOTES:

THURSDAY

EQ/ I CAN NOTES:

FRIDAY

EQ/ I CAN NOTES:

READING *Tracker*

CLASS:

BOOK TITLE: AUTHOR:

DATE	STUDENT	PAGES READ	NOTES

LESSON *Planner*

SUBJECT:

UNIT:

LESSON:

DATE:

OBJECTIVE:

OVERVIEW

TOPICS COVERED

ASSIGNMENTS

NOTES

DAY PLANNER *Monday*

DATE:

5am:

6am:

7am:

8am:

9am:

10am:

11am:

12pm:

1pm:

2pm:

3pm:

4pm:

DAILY TO DO LIST:

DAILY GOALS:

NOTES & REMINDERS:

DAY PLANNER *Tuesday*

DATE:

5am:

6am:

7am:

8am:

9am:

10am:

11am:

12pm:

1pm:

2pm:

3pm:

4pm:

DAILY TO DO LIST:

DAILY GOALS:

NOTES & REMINDERS:

DAY PLANNER *Wednesday*

DATE:

5am:

6am:

7am:

8am:

9am:

10am:

11am:

12pm:

1pm:

2pm:

3pm:

4pm:

DAILY TO DO LIST:

DAILY GOALS:

NOTES & REMINDERS:

DAY PLANNER *Thursday*

DATE:

5am:

6am:

7am:

8am:

9am:

10am:

11am:

12pm:

1pm:

2pm:

3pm:

4pm:

DAILY TO DO LIST:

DAILY GOALS:

NOTES & REMINDERS:

DAY PLANNER

DATE:

5am:

6am:

7am:

8am:

9am:

10am:

11am:

12pm:

1pm:

2pm:

3pm:

4pm:

DAILY TO DO LIST:

DAILY GOALS:

NOTES & REMINDERS:

DATE:

WEEKLY ROLL *Call*

FIRST NAME: LAST NAME: STATUS:

WEEKLY *Overview*

WEEK OF: ....

MONDAY

TUESDAY

WEDNESDAY

THURSDAY

FRIDAY

SATURDAY

SUNDAY

IMPORTANT NOTES

WEEKLY *Lesson Plan*

MONDAY

EQ/ I CAN NOTES:

TUESDAY

EQ/ I CAN NOTES:

WEDNESDAY

EQ/ I CAN NOTES:

THURSDAY

EQ/ I CAN NOTES:

FRIDAY

EQ/ I CAN NOTES:

READING *Tracker*

CLASS:

BOOK TITLE: AUTHOR:

DATE	STUDENT	PAGES READ	NOTES

LESSON *Planner*

SUBJECT:

UNIT:

LESSON:

DATE:

OBJECTIVE:

OVERVIEW

TOPICS COVERED

ASSIGNMENTS

NOTES

DAY PLANNER *Monday*

DATE:

DAILY TO DO LIST:

5am:

6am:

7am:

8am: **DAILY GOALS:**

9am:

10am:

11am:

          NOTES & REMINDERS:

12pm:

1pm:

2pm:

3pm:

4pm:

DAY PLANNER

DATE:

5am:

6am:

7am:

8am:

9am:

10am:

11am:

12pm:

1pm:

2pm:

3pm:

4pm:

DAILY TO DO LIST:

DAILY GOALS:

NOTES & REMINDERS:

DAY PLANNER *Wednesday*

DATE:

5am:

6am:

7am:

8am:

9am:

10am:

11am:

12pm:

1pm:

2pm:

3pm:

4pm:

DAILY TO DO LIST:

DAILY GOALS:

NOTES & REMINDERS:

DAY PLANNER *Thursday*

DATE:

DAILY TO DO LIST:

5am:

6am:

7am:

8am:
                                              DAILY GOALS:

9am:

10am:

11am:

NOTES & REMINDERS:

12pm:

1pm:

2pm:

3pm:

4pm:

DAY PLANNER

DATE:

5am:

6am:

7am:

8am:

9am:

10am:

11am:

12pm:

1pm:

2pm:

3pm:

4pm:

DAILY TO DO LIST:

DAILY GOALS:

NOTES & REMINDERS:

DATE:

WEEKLY ROLL *Call*

FIRST NAME: LAST NAME: STATUS:

WEEKLY *Overview*

WEEK OF: ....

MONDAY

TUESDAY

WEDNESDAY

THURSDAY

FRIDAY

SATURDAY

SUNDAY

IMPORTANT NOTES

WEEKLY *Lesson Plan*

MONDAY

EQ/ I CAN NOTES:

TUESDAY

EQ/ I CAN NOTES:

WEDNESDAY

EQ/ I CAN NOTES:

THURSDAY

EQ/ I CAN NOTES:

FRIDAY

EQ/ I CAN NOTES:

READING *Tracker*

CLASS:

BOOK TITLE: AUTHOR:

DATE	STUDENT	PAGES READ	NOTES

LESSON *Planner*

SUBJECT:

UNIT:

LESSON:

DATE:

OBJECTIVE:

OVERVIEW

TOPICS COVERED

ASSIGNMENTS

NOTES

DAY PLANNER *Monday*

DATE:

5am:

6am:

7am:

8am:

9am:

10am:

11am:

12pm:

1pm:

2pm:

3pm:

4pm:

DAILY TO DO LIST:

DAILY GOALS:

NOTES & REMINDERS:

DAY PLANNER

DATE:

5am:

6am:

7am:

8am:

9am:

10am:

11am:

12pm:

1pm:

2pm:

3pm:

4pm:

DAILY TO DO LIST:

DAILY GOALS:

NOTES & REMINDERS:

DAY PLANNER *Wednesday*

DATE:

5am:

6am:

7am:

8am:

9am:

10am:

11am:

12pm:

1pm:

2pm:

3pm:

4pm:

DAILY TO DO LIST:

DAILY GOALS:

NOTES & REMINDERS:

DAY PLANNER *Thursday*

DATE:

5am:

6am:

7am:

8am:

9am:

10am:

11am:

12pm:

1pm:

2pm:

3pm:

4pm:

DAILY TO DO LIST:

DAILY GOALS:

NOTES & REMINDERS:

DAY PLANNER

DATE:

5am:

6am:

7am:

8am:

9am:

10am:

11am:

12pm:

1pm:

2pm:

3pm:

4pm:

DAILY TO DO LIST:

DAILY GOALS:

NOTES & REMINDERS:

DATE:

WEEKLY ROLL *Call*

FIRST NAME: LAST NAME: STATUS:

WEEKLY *Overview*

WEEK OF: ....

MONDAY	TUESDAY	WEDNESDAY

THURSDAY	FRIDAY	SATURDAY

SUNDAY

IMPORTANT NOTES

WEEKLY *Lesson Plan*

MONDAY

EQ/ I CAN NOTES:

TUESDAY

EQ/ I CAN NOTES:

WEDNESDAY

EQ/ I CAN NOTES:

THURSDAY

EQ/ I CAN NOTES:

FRIDAY

EQ/ I CAN NOTES:

READING *Tracker*

CLASS:

BOOK TITLE: AUTHOR:

DATE	STUDENT	PAGES READ	NOTES

LESSON *Planner*

SUBJECT:

UNIT:

LESSON:

DATE:

OBJECTIVE:

OVERVIEW

TOPICS COVERED

ASSIGNMENTS

NOTES

DAY PLANNER *Monday*

DATE:

5am:

6am:

7am:

8am:

9am:

10am:

11am:

12pm:

1pm:

2pm:

3pm:

4pm:

DAILY TO DO LIST:

DAILY GOALS:

NOTES & REMINDERS:

DAY PLANNER  Tuesday

DATE: | **DAILY TO DO LIST:**

5am:

6am:

7am:

8am:

DAILY GOALS:

9am:

10am:

11am:

NOTES & REMINDERS:

12pm:

1pm:

2pm:

3pm:

4pm:

DAY PLANNER *Wednesday*

DATE:

5am:

6am:

7am:

8am:

9am:

10am:

11am:

12pm:

1pm:

2pm:

3pm:

4pm:

DAILY TO DO LIST:

DAILY GOALS:

NOTES & REMINDERS:

DAY PLANNER *Thursday*

DATE:

DAILY TO DO LIST:

5am:

6am:

7am:

8am: **DAILY GOALS:**

9am:

10am:

11am: **NOTES & REMINDERS:**

12pm:

1pm:

2pm:

3pm:

4pm:

DAY PLANNER

DATE:

5am:

6am:

7am:

8am:

9am:

10am:

11am:

12pm:

1pm:

2pm:

3pm:

4pm:

DAILY TO DO LIST:

DAILY GOALS:

NOTES & REMINDERS:

DATE:

WEEKLY ROLL *Call*

FIRST NAME: LAST NAME: STATUS:

WEEKLY *Overview*

WEEK OF: ....

MONDAY

TUESDAY

WEDNESDAY

THURSDAY

FRIDAY

SATURDAY

SUNDAY

IMPORTANT NOTES

WEEKLY *Lesson Plan*

MONDAY

EQ/ I CAN NOTES:

TUESDAY

EQ/ I CAN NOTES:

WEDNESDAY

EQ/ I CAN NOTES:

THURSDAY

EQ/ I CAN NOTES:

FRIDAY

EQ/ I CAN NOTES:

READING *Tracker*

CLASS:

BOOK TITLE: AUTHOR:

DATE	STUDENT	PAGES READ	NOTES

LESSON *Planner*

SUBJECT:

UNIT:

LESSON:

DATE:

OBJECTIVE:

OVERVIEW

TOPICS COVERED

ASSIGNMENTS

NOTES

DAY PLANNER *Monday*

DATE:

5am:

6am:

7am:

8am:

9am:

10am:

11am:

12pm:

1pm:

2pm:

3pm:

4pm:

DAILY TO DO LIST:

DAILY GOALS:

NOTES & REMINDERS:

DAY PLANNER

DATE:

5am:

6am:

7am:

8am:

9am:

10am:

11am:

12pm:

1pm:

2pm:

3pm:

4pm:

DAILY TO DO LIST:

DAILY GOALS:

NOTES & REMINDERS:

DAY PLANNER *Wednesday*

DATE:

5am:

6am:

7am:

8am:

9am:

10am:

11am:

12pm:

1pm:

2pm:

3pm:

4pm:

DAILY TO DO LIST:

DAILY GOALS:

NOTES & REMINDERS:

DAY PLANNER *Thursday*

DATE:

5am:

6am:

7am:

8am:

9am:

10am:

11am:

12pm:

1pm:

2pm:

3pm:

4pm:

DAILY TO DO LIST:

DAILY GOALS:

NOTES & REMINDERS:

DAY PLANNER

DATE:

5am:

6am:

7am:

8am:

9am:

10am:

11am:

12pm:

1pm:

2pm:

3pm:

4pm:

DAILY TO DO LIST:

DAILY GOALS:

NOTES & REMINDERS:

DATE:

WEEKLY ROLL *Call*

FIRST NAME: LAST NAME: STATUS:

WEEKLY *Overview*

WEEK OF: ....

MONDAY

TUESDAY

WEDNESDAY

THURSDAY

FRIDAY

SATURDAY

SUNDAY

IMPORTANT NOTES

WEEKLY *Lesson Plan*

MONDAY

EQ/ I CAN NOTES:

TUESDAY

EQ/ I CAN NOTES:

WEDNESDAY

EQ/ I CAN NOTES:

THURSDAY

EQ/ I CAN NOTES:

FRIDAY

EQ/ I CAN NOTES:

READING *Tracker*

CLASS: _____

BOOK TITLE: _____   **AUTHOR:** _____

DATE	STUDENT	PAGES READ	NOTES

LESSON *Planner*

SUBJECT:

UNIT:

LESSON:

DATE:

OBJECTIVE:

OVERVIEW

TOPICS COVERED

ASSIGNMENTS

NOTES

DAY PLANNER *Monday*

DATE:

5am:

6am:

7am:

8am:

9am:

10am:

11am:

12pm:

1pm:

2pm:

3pm:

4pm:

DAILY TO DO LIST:

DAILY GOALS:

NOTES & REMINDERS:

DAY PLANNER

DATE:

5am:

6am:

7am:

8am:

9am:

10am:

11am:

12pm:

1pm:

2pm:

3pm:

4pm:

DAILY TO DO LIST:

DAILY GOALS:

NOTES & REMINDERS:

DAY PLANNER *Wednesday*

DATE:

5am:

6am:

7am:

8am:

9am:

10am:

11am:

12pm:

1pm:

2pm:

3pm:

4pm:

DAILY TO DO LIST:

DAILY GOALS:

NOTES & REMINDERS:

DAY PLANNER *Thursday*

DATE:

5am:

6am:

7am:

8am:

9am:

10am:

11am:

12pm:

1pm:

2pm:

3pm:

4pm:

DAILY TO DO LIST:

DAILY GOALS:

NOTES & REMINDERS:

DAY PLANNER

DATE:

5am:

6am:

7am:

8am:

9am:

10am:

11am:

12pm:

1pm:

2pm:

3pm:

4pm:

DAILY TO DO LIST:

DAILY GOALS:

NOTES & REMINDERS:

DATE:

WEEKLY ROLL *Call*

FIRST NAME: LAST NAME: STATUS:

WEEKLY *Overview*

WEEK OF: ....

MONDAY

TUESDAY

WEDNESDAY

THURSDAY

FRIDAY

SATURDAY

SUNDAY

IMPORTANT NOTES

WEEKLY *Lesson Plan*

MONDAY

EQ/ I CAN NOTES:

TUESDAY

EQ/ I CAN NOTES:

WEDNESDAY

EQ/ I CAN NOTES:

THURSDAY

EQ/ I CAN NOTES:

FRIDAY

EQ/ I CAN NOTES:

READING *Tracker*

CLASS: ....

BOOK TITLE: ....   AUTHOR: ....

DATE	STUDENT	PAGES READ	NOTES

LESSON *Planner*

SUBJECT:

UNIT:

LESSON:

DATE:

OBJECTIVE:

OVERVIEW

TOPICS COVERED

ASSIGNMENTS

NOTES

DAY PLANNER *Monday*

DATE:

DAILY TO DO LIST:

5am:

6am:

7am:

8am: **DAILY GOALS:**

9am:

10am:

11am:

NOTES & REMINDERS:

12pm:

1pm:

2pm:

3pm:

4pm:

DAY PLANNER

DATE:

5am:

6am:

7am:

8am:

9am:

10am:

11am:

12pm:

1pm:

2pm:

3pm:

4pm:

DAILY TO DO LIST:

DAILY GOALS:

NOTES & REMINDERS:

DAY PLANNER *Wednesday*

DATE:

5am:

6am:

7am:

8am:

9am:

10am:

11am:

12pm:

1pm:

2pm:

3pm:

4pm:

DAILY TO DO LIST:

DAILY GOALS:

NOTES & REMINDERS:

DAY PLANNER *Thursday*

DATE:

5am:

6am:

7am:

8am:

9am:

10am:

11am:

12pm:

1pm:

2pm:

3pm:

4pm:

DAILY TO DO LIST:

DAILY GOALS:

NOTES & REMINDERS:

DAY PLANNER

DATE:

5am:

6am:

7am:

8am:

9am:

10am:

11am:

12pm:

1pm:

2pm:

3pm:

4pm:

DAILY TO DO LIST:

DAILY GOALS:

NOTES & REMINDERS:

PARENT-TEACHER *Meetings*

STUDENT NAME:

DATE & TIME:

REASON FOR MEETING

TOPICS DISCUSSED

ACTION PLAN & GOALS

STUDENT NAME:

DATE & TIME:

REASON FOR MEETING

TOPICS DISCUSSED

ACTION PLAN & GOALS

STUDENT *Information*

STUDENT INFORMATION

NAME: BIRTH DATE:

ADDRESS: PARENTS NAMES:

PHONE: EMAIL ADDRESS:

ACADEMIC HISTORY   ### MEDICAL INFORMATION

STUDENT ID:

CHALLENGES:

STRENGTHS:

PRIMARY CONTACT INFORMATION   ### EMERGENCY CONTACT INFORMATION

ADDITIONAL INFORMATION

STUDENT *Information*

STUDENT INFORMATION

NAME: ....

ADDRESS: ....

PHONE: ....

BIRTH DATE: ....

PARENTS NAMES: ....

EMAIL ADDRESS: ....

ACADEMIC HISTORY

STUDENT ID: ....

CHALLENGES: ....

STRENGTHS: ....

MEDICAL INFORMATION

PRIMARY CONTACT INFORMATION

EMERGENCY CONTACT INFORMATION

ADDITIONAL INFORMATION

STUDENT *Information*

STUDENT INFORMATION

NAME: BIRTH DATE:

ADDRESS: PARENTS NAMES:

PHONE: EMAIL ADDRESS:

ACADEMIC HISTORY   ### MEDICAL INFORMATION

STUDENT ID:

CHALLENGES:

STRENGTHS:

PRIMARY CONTACT INFORMATION   ### EMERGENCY CONTACT INFORMATION

ADDITIONAL INFORMATION

STUDENT *Information*

STUDENT INFORMATION

NAME: BIRTH DATE:

ADDRESS: PARENTS NAMES:

PHONE: EMAIL ADDRESS:

ACADEMIC HISTORY   ### MEDICAL INFORMATION

STUDENT ID:

CHALLENGES:

STRENGTHS:

PRIMARY CONTACT INFORMATION   ### EMERGENCY CONTACT INFORMATION

ADDITIONAL INFORMATION

STUDENT *Information*

STUDENT INFORMATION

NAME:

ADDRESS:

PHONE:

BIRTH DATE:

PARENTS NAMES:

EMAIL ADDRESS:

ACADEMIC HISTORY

STUDENT ID:

CHALLENGES:

STRENGTHS:

MEDICAL INFORMATION

PRIMARY CONTACT INFORMATION

EMERGENCY CONTACT INFORMATION

ADDITIONAL INFORMATION

STUDENT *Information*

STUDENT INFORMATION

NAME: _____

ADDRESS: _____

PHONE: _____

BIRTH DATE: _____

PARENTS NAMES: _____

EMAIL ADDRESS: _____

ACADEMIC HISTORY

STUDENT ID:

CHALLENGES:

STRENGTHS:

MEDICAL INFORMATION

PRIMARY CONTACT INFORMATION

EMERGENCY CONTACT INFORMATION

ADDITIONAL INFORMATION

STUDENT *Information*

STUDENT INFORMATION

NAME:

ADDRESS:

PHONE:

BIRTH DATE:

PARENTS NAMES:

EMAIL ADDRESS:

ACADEMIC HISTORY

STUDENT ID:

CHALLENGES:

STRENGTHS:

MEDICAL INFORMATION

PRIMARY CONTACT INFORMATION

EMERGENCY CONTACT INFORMATION

ADDITIONAL INFORMATION

STUDENT *Information*

STUDENT INFORMATION

NAME: _____   BIRTH DATE: _____

ADDRESS: _____   PARENTS NAMES: _____

PHONE: _____   EMAIL ADDRESS: _____

ACADEMIC HISTORY

STUDENT ID: _____

CHALLENGES: _____

STRENGTHS: _____

MEDICAL INFORMATION

PRIMARY CONTACT INFORMATION

EMERGENCY CONTACT INFORMATION

ADDITIONAL INFORMATION

STUDENT *Information*

STUDENT INFORMATION

NAME:

ADDRESS:

PHONE:

BIRTH DATE:

PARENTS NAMES:

EMAIL ADDRESS:

ACADEMIC HISTORY

STUDENT ID:

CHALLENGES:

STRENGTHS:

MEDICAL INFORMATION

PRIMARY CONTACT INFORMATION

EMERGENCY CONTACT INFORMATION

ADDITIONAL INFORMATION

STUDENT Information

STUDENT INFORMATION

NAME:

ADDRESS:

PHONE:

BIRTH DATE:

PARENTS NAMES:

EMAIL ADDRESS:

ACADEMIC HISTORY

STUDENT ID:

CHALLENGES:

STRENGTHS:

MEDICAL INFORMATION

PRIMARY CONTACT INFORMATION

EMERGENCY CONTACT INFORMATION

ADDITIONAL INFORMATION

STUDENT *Information*

STUDENT INFORMATION

NAME:

ADDRESS:

PHONE:

BIRTH DATE:

PARENTS NAMES:

EMAIL ADDRESS:

ACADEMIC HISTORY

STUDENT ID:

CHALLENGES:

STRENGTHS:

MEDICAL INFORMATION

PRIMARY CONTACT INFORMATION

EMERGENCY CONTACT INFORMATION

ADDITIONAL INFORMATION

STUDENT *Information*

STUDENT INFORMATION

NAME: BIRTH DATE:

ADDRESS: PARENTS NAMES:

PHONE: EMAIL ADDRESS:

ACADEMIC HISTORY   ### MEDICAL INFORMATION

STUDENT ID:

CHALLENGES:

STRENGTHS:

PRIMARY CONTACT INFORMATION   ### EMERGENCY CONTACT INFORMATION

ADDITIONAL INFORMATION

Made in the USA
Coppell, TX
11 June 2022

78713897R00083